Rethinking Repair

poems by

Monica Rentfrow

Finishing Line Press
Georgetown, Kentucky

Rethinking Repair

For Monica.
Your voice matters,
and it lives on forever in these poems.

Copyright © 2020 by Monica Rentfrow
ISBN 978-1-64662-231-3 First Edition
All rights reserved under International and Pan-American Copyright Conventions. No part of this book may be reproduced in any manner whatsoever without written permission from the publisher, except in the case of brief quotations embodied in critical articles and reviews.

ACKNOWLEDGMENTS

Sincere thanks to the many mentors and friends who have given their time, energy, support, and love to Monica throughout her life, and particularly to her family and to the love of her life, Roy Cargill.

For their guidance and mentorship in her development as a writer, special thanks to Bill Palmer, Robert Vivian, John Rybicki, Ted Kooser, Hilda Raz, and Grace Bauer.

This publication would not be possible without the work of Bill Palmer, who prepared the manuscript for submission, Laura von Wallmenich who prepared the final manuscript and cover art, and most of all, Tracie and Ed Massar, who were committed to bringing Monica's work to the world.

Three of the poems in this collection were previously published in 2018 in *Wordgathering: A Journal of Disability Poetry and Literature*: "Spondyloepiphyseal Dysplasia Congenita," "The Bone Room," and "Short Rules."

Funded in part by Finishing Line Press' One Last Word Program.

Publisher: Leah Maines
Editor: Christen Kincaid
Cover Art: AdobeStock
Author Photos: Ed Massar
Cover Design: Laura von Wallmenich

Printed in the USA on acid-free paper.
Order online: www.finishinglinepress.com
also available on amazon.com

Author inquiries and mail orders:
Finishing Line Press
P. O. Box 1626
Georgetown, Kentucky 40324
U. S. A.

Table of Contents

Introduction ix
Author's Foreword xi

SECTION I: THE BODY

Another S.E.D.c. Scratch 1
Anesthetic Awakening 2
Little Victories 3
My Halo 4
Daily Practice 5
Semi 6
Metal 7
Stakes 8
Spondyloepiphyseal Dysplasia Congenita 9
The Bone Room 10

SECTION II: THE FAMILY

Population Control 11
What to Keep in a Kangaroo Pouch 12
Nuts for My Sister 13
Tender 14
Contemplating College Majors 15
I Aim… 16
The Bookshoppe & Superior Perk 17
Putting a Spin on Things 18
Google Midgets 19
A Minute Ago 20
Story of My Life 21
The Pine 22

Forgotten 23
Hypotheticals 24
Presbyterian Disaster Assistance 25
Labor Day Weekends at Lakeview United Methodist
    Campground 26
Gelston Hall 150 27

SECTION 3: THE EVERYDAY

Routine.. 28
6-seater Cessna 29
Reflecting on My Place in the Cosmos................... 30
Putty Syringed into Outer Ear Will Harden 31
Short Rules 32
The Gait Lab 33
Ty 3 34
The Red Box 35
I, Your Shield... 36
My Halo Has Shifted 37
Those Little Reminders.. 38
Rethinking Repair 39

INTRODUCTION
Amanda Massar

Imagine laying in soft damp grass, surrounded by deep navy blue. The suede night sky pierced with pin holes in pleasing, random patterns of dazzling white-gold. Subtle hushed words exchanged with a friend, a sister—as though having a raised voice would make the fragile light from the stars shy away from view.

Imagine you see something remarkable in that sky, a glitter of blue perhaps, a shape made in the array of dots, or maybe something flashing strangely that makes you question the existence of life Out There. You say to your companion, "Check that out, do you see that?" and you point with a frantic, excited finger out into the utter vastness of space.

There is a distance between your eyes and that of your friends, and you know this, so you try to do some perspective correction by placing your face as close to theirs as you can. You point again, but it isn't quite working yet. You take their finger and try to align it with yours, taking into consideration the angle of their body as it differs from your own. It isn't even really about the thing you saw anymore; it is about the challenge of making sure they see it, too… You scour the sky with their pointer, thinking that if their finger can find it, their eyes are sure to follow—and then maybe they will see what you see. After trying for what seems like too long, it happens. "Oh yeah, I see it!" At first you think they're just being nice or maybe wanting to stop the hunt, so you skeptically ask them to describe it, and they do, and you look at their eyes to gauge truthfulness. Yes, they really do. A feeling of pride and satisfaction fills your lungs along with crisp dark air. You two had a moment of shared awe, likeness of mind, a human connection fueling a desire within our very nature... even for just a moment.

My memories are full of moments like this, small moments that speak to how my sister saw the world. Every person has a unique vantagepoint which is the result of our singular experience navigating this life. No two humans will ever peer from the very same lens; it is an impossibility, but a writer must believe in the power of words to bridge the gap between us. My sister, Monica Kathleen Rentfrow, was a writer and a poet, and she spent immeasurable hours of her extraordinary life understanding the lenses through which we see the world.

Monica's vantagepoint was on the exceptional end of the spectrum. Measuring 3 feet and 1 inch, she stood at the belt loops of most people her age. Though her height was her most noticeable characteristic, it was not who she was; however, Monica learned over time, and with trial and effort, to turn this feature into a way to engage others, change perspectives, and make strides toward fulfilling a goal of shared human experience.

Monica was infinitely interested in other people's perspectives. She would ask a question and would intently listen while you gave your response, with a look in her eyes like she was searching through an internal database for similarities between your reply and her own basis of understanding. She was only too happy to share in the triumph when she found a likeness between you, similar to the feeling of both sets of two peoples eyes coming to rest on the same flashing spot in the extensive night sky while stargazing. She would light up. In that moment the space between two unique perspectives would grow smaller. Normalizing and humanizing all people, regardless of physical form, was one of Monica's passions.

Writing held special power for her. She wrote with a fierce authenticity, pointing ceaselessly at the profoundly human core that allows her readers to see, if just for a moment, glimpses of the night sky from her own perspective.

Author's Foreward

Rethinking Repair is a semi-autobiographical collection of serious and humorous poetic works that explores effects a body with dwarfism has had on one individual.

Most of the poems lean on a precise moment when dwarfism—a rare medical condition present at birth—directly has influenced the emotion or outcome of a situation. Conversely, I illuminate moments when dwarfism has had absolutely no direct influence on my experiences; I do this to counterbalance the possible perception or belief that all the experiences in my life center on dwarfism. Indeed many poems are simple displays of managing the "repair" of familial and everyday stresses. In this way, the collection serves as an example of an unusual life experience. Because it focuses on the realities and exigencies of living with dwarfism, this narrative on repair is a crucial addition to the discourse of diversity studies. More specifically, this collection will further the discourse of dwarfism in literature. The poems collected in *Rethinking Repair* are organized in three sections— each of which contains poems that center on the concept of repair to the body, the family, and the mitigation of everyday stresses. Poetic influences include such poets as Mary Oliver, Ted Kooser, Paul Guest, and James Cihlar; professorial influence includes Ted Kooser, Hilda Raz, and Grace Bauer.

SECTION I: THE BODY

Another S.E.D.c. Scratch[1]

> *"The opposite of beauty is not ugliness, it is injury."*
> —Greg Hewitt, *The Eros Conspiracy*

Metal can save a life
so can blood   and bone.

I didn't know during recess that
my uncle leaves work
to have a needle stuck in his arm
so does mom,
my grandparents

A week later part of them
becomes part of me
in a bright, cold room
as my neck learns how to be strong
with the help of dead man bone,
mashed shavings from my shins,
wire-bent bits,
and a dash of grace

---

[1] S.E.D.c.— Spondyloepiphyseal dysplasia congenital, a rare bone growth disorder, caused Monica's type of dwarfism.

Anesthetic Awakening

it's a strange thing to lose three days,
                wake with a cry, like rebirth

suddenly what you knew is new
                blinking in this: a re-formed you

a desire to overturn tables
                bubbles through blood

to rise from this bed of clotting cement,
                pluck plastic tubes, lasso freedom

crash and thrash through walls,
                this Bigfoot being of you

Little Victories

After five months flat in bed
as bones healed at the base of my head
the doctor removed the stabilizing pins
that pierced the first layer of skull skin.
It would be unwise to sit, they said,
without a therapist. But when Mom sped
to fetch my snack, a desire set in
to rise by myself—and, boy, I would win.
Hand gripping rail, I threw a leg (dead
muscled) over the edge, the second as first led,
and sat there committing a hospital sin
while the world refused to stop the spin.
Mom came back and nearly dropped her cup;
when asked what I was doing, I said: "Sitting up!"

My Halo

I grew stronger in my neck
where the doctor stuffed in
bone and tiny wire
drilled four pins
into my head one-eighth inch
while I was asleep
puncturing little holes
in my forehead and under my hair

The four bars threaded down my front and back
to join with a cast around the torso
except for the cut out crater
where I could reach through
thin, stretchy fabric to scratch around my navel.

For five months I lay on my bed in the living room
to watch Power Rangers on my side
sleep on my front, the bed four inches from my eyes
do homework on my back with triangle-prism glasses
poop into a bedpan with a towel across my waist
lying in my halo around our house,
too awkward to slide me into a car

Daily Practice

busy checking a check of a fat-forties man
who's just left, she doesn't see me, next in line

I'd like to pound with bare fists on the counter wall
or chuck a pen at her forehead

but I hang back a few feet, put on the practiced grin,
pretend I'm wanting not to disrupt this grand work

Semi

I did it because I could,
because I was scared to do it,
and because it was there—
resting between yellow-painted lines,
its gigantic round feet, long-stretched body,
eyelids holding back the glare,
and silence that chilled my toes.
I double-checked the head, to be sure it was asleep,
then made for it, dashing under the hollow,
metal belly. There was space enough but I ducked anyway.
I did not look up until I breathed on the other side
and lived to tell the tale.

Metal

I.
paper clip
bracelet
notebook binding
handcuffs
screws
plates/shunts
electrical wiring center
piping
silverware
scaffolds
sheet metal
factory machinery
blood content
water purifier
elevator handrail

        II.
        the way it bends to the mind
        natural resource made unnatural
        shape-slammed to make tools that shape-slam
        shrieking sound of laser cutting
        requires goggles, lead-weight gloves
        reflects light to capture pictures
        holds time in its place
        prints paper, templates, person x-rays
        cuts what shouldn't be cut
        brainless follower of controls by another
        fulfills purpose of solidity and strength

III.
piping shrieks to the sound of laser cutting what shouldn't be cut . . . handcuffed, holding time in its place . . . a brainless follower of controls from another . . . silverware prints on paper templates . . . personal x-rays require goggles . . . lead-weight gloves to make tools that shape sheet metal the way it bends to the mind . . . reflecting light to capture pictures of blood controls . . . natural resource made unnatural

Stakes

I was lying on the hard white table top, the pins like not yet rusted stakes of a country fence jamming out of my knee and ankle. For reasons I do not remember I could not be given anesthetic. My insides shook like a burp in the Grand Canyon.

A man came in with bolt cutters as big as a German Shepherd hidden behind his back. He approached the left side of the table while I tried to focus on the ceiling tile with the painted happy butterfly.

I could see the one leg of the cutters at attention in the air. I closed my eyes.

Spondyloepiphyseal Dysplasia Congenita

I don't really like babies
but the young SEDs get me
every time
the way they stagger
with limbs they may never grow into
on hips that contain not an ounce
of bone
chattering in high octaves
and pushing themselves back up
from the floor
chasing others twice their size
Shortcutting under tables with no need
to duck head

Once, sitting on the side
of a crowd, I saw a girl of three,
very small,
padding about, darting from one
side to the other, weaving through legs
like corn stalks
while parents sat by
seemingly cooler than the cucumber
on my lunch plate
and I just about pulled a superhero stunt
before I realized I did just the same
at her age

The Bone Room

My doctor's secretary walks
to the door of The Bone
Room, turns a key in
an old metal lock. Only
a teenager, I do not know
what Laura is offering me.

I am admitted to a room
full of bone bits and wholes
on thin wooden shelves,
in cabinets behind dusty
glass doors. Missing bodies' hands,
joints, clubfeet, a pelvis, a cranium
enlarged from achondroplasia.
It is like a history
of my ancestors, my people.
I look but do not touch.

I turn around
and there it is: a whole
skeleton, complete with scoliosis.
Missing eyes, missing spirit—
it hangs in its case.
My feet grow roots
and my ears fold in
on themselves as Laura
recites facts, smiling.
It was such a structure
that if my skin and muscle were to fall
away it would be me
standing forever in a glass display.
I could be a sacrifice to science.

Section II: The Family

Population Control

you always want two caterpillars
she says on the day I learn to pluck weeds

I'm warned to *never let them kiss*
because they might get too attached
as I take from her palm
the tiny pruning tool,
turn to the mirror

I hear *that's why we take out*
some of their legs every week

I lean into the wall
the way I've seen her tilt,
press belly-gut to granite—
when I wince she smiles:
a leg falls in the sink

I look for the hole, shocked
that I can't find the wound

even when she flips on the vanity
to *draw those bugs out—don't*
forget that light scares them still
as my hand raises for round two
in this fight of face gardening

later, looking at the finished job, I wonder
when the lady bug popping lessons will begin

What to Keep in a Kangaroo Pouch

toothbrush
water bottle

extra shower soap
a change of clothes

neck pillows
campfire logs

a guitar
some stars

quilt from our bed
brown sack breakfast

the keys you forgot
on the way out the door

Nuts for My Sister

I took you a crunchy
peanut butter sandwich
today while you worked—
nuts of love bulging
the slices of bread

I wrapped it in a napkin,
then another and another,
securing the wrapped sides
with tape, as I wish
I could you

I brought you also
a few small bars of chocolate,
as if its sugar
could make your world sweeter

Tender

I would swear
it was my father's favorite
word. I'd hear
it almost every dinnertime,
how tender the meat was.
Pork, beef, turkey,
and the venison he'd shot
the week before: it was
all tender, any way he cooked it.

I do not hate meat,
but I do not like most
besides ham and seafood.
My father hardly ever ate seafood.

What he didn't know was
that if he weren't in the kitchen
counting how many of the "agreed"
bites I'd eat, my baby sister
was reaching across plates
bite after tender bite.

Contemplating College Majors

I noticed my father
when we drank coffee
in brown chairs
on his cement patio,
the sun beat against
the cold breeze
on our skin, pleased
as much as I
at the sight, a moment
of soft words and smiles
when I learned
that even mean men
can be sweet in stillness

I Aim…

Afraid of backfire throwing me on my butt, I instinctively lock elbows, close my eyes, pretend I can shut my ears. My great-grandfather's pistol is cold and foreign to me, though not my father. I think of his first shot, about my age, Grandpa watching nearby to see if his directions were followed. Perhaps my father closed only one eye. My eyes snap open at the shot to see dirt spring up where my bullet landed. I am surprised to find the world unchanged. I smile. My father is smiling. Maybe Grandpa smiles above the clouds. I look across the dirt ditch—one of many on my father's land behind his ranch-style house. I look at the milk jugs, glad they are not birds or other prey my father hunts with his rifles. I raise the gun. I aim this time. I miss. I aim again. No dust cloud this time.

The Bookshoppe & Superior Perk

for Lisa

The door chimes as I push
into my place, walking down
the slant of spotted cement
—the floor of a once hardware shop.

I hear the familiar hello
as I pass red couches, books
on thin metal shelves, wicker
tables where sandwiches slowly disappear.

Lisa talks about her two boys,
one in Australia. She suggests a good
book she's read, looks up a title
I seek. We smile over an old joke.

If Anne were working she'd talk
about biking to work. Barb, her granddaughter.
All three ask how classes and other
friends are getting along this week.

Streetlight lies on the counter
from the big front windows
where I pick up a fat, baby
blue mug of chai only Lisa can make.

I sit, cross ankles, sip,
watch water fall from the green
awning to the sidewalk, feel
warm sliding down a throat to a tired body.

Putting a Spin on Things

for Lin

Was it your idea
or mine to take
the world into our hands
close our eyes
feel the rise and fall
of mountains, oceans,
countless countries
spinning out of control
under our fingertips,
the whole Earth painted
in crayon colors

suddenly the world stopped
and I would lift my pointer
to read the black print
of foreign lands: Sri Lanka,
Czechoslovakia, San Francisco

sometimes we'd spin
again, peeking through closed
lids, until we landed on one
our tongue didn't trip on,
while we knew any place would
be better than being here
and neither of us said it

Google Midgets

Bridget the Midget
Eric the Midget
Midget fight on Springer
Hire a midget
Rent a midget.com
Japanese Midget Submarine
A tiny sub-species of the human race.

> Mainly raised in midget mills,
> for the entertainment of normal people.

Midget madness
Easy midget
Midget hand job
North Eastern Midget Association
Midget Motors Supply
The Midget Manifesto. Proposal:

> Harness the inherent power of midgets to provide clean,
> reliable energy, and a source of entertainment for mankind.

Quarter Midget racing for kids
Midget Throwing: A Lost Art
Wonder Midget
Modest Midget

For over a decade, I dreamt of fucking a midget

An extremely small person who is otherwise normally proportioned: offensive.

A Minute Ago

a guy winked
at me downtown
it was not the sort of wink
that awakens butterflies
in my stomach
but, rather, the kind
that feels like a spider
crawled out of your crotch

Story of My Life

I am paper
reams and reams of it
paragraphs stuck
in my armpits and flab
I wish weren't back there,
lodged in hair
roots, bulging
at the seam where my
rib was spared, stitched
in the button holes
of my legs, clamped in,
bound, deep
in my spine

The Pine

undisturbed by a loud landworld
dozens of ducks sleep
in the evening sun
on quiet waves
with curled necks tucked
in warm silhouette feathers

Forgotten

it's raining like the sound
of two keyboards being typed upon
but you've lost the ability to listen
after all this time spent sliding
windows shut and cursing
forgotten umbrellas

forgotten are the days of puddle
seeking and climbing dark tree bark
to sip from leaf bowls while yellow
peeks between the clouds

no, now there are meetings to run,
clocks to race, and ladders to climb instead
alternating hand and foot to move
up instead of forward

Hypotheticals

if I could choose
the body & being
of my next life
I'd be
a lightning bug:
though my wings
might be bent a bit
or legs squashed
from a small hand
cupping me out
of the night air,
and maybe even forget
to breathe
inside an old jar, it'd be
worth it to see close up
the light in the smile of this child

Presbyterian Disaster Assistance

No hammer was holstered
or pipe laid or wire connected
but we had maps of neighborhoods
to canvas, all with a door to knock on
and flash our badges proving
we were not looters or others unwanted

we sat on couches, pointed at shingles,
walked through rooms to survey Katrina's
damage, writing down which mechanics
needed to stop at this house

mostly though, we drank lots
of tea, gave hugs,
listened to stories that wrung
our hearts, and heard thanks
for sacrificed spring breaks

no hammer was holstered
or pipe laid or wire connected
except those within ourselves
at the end of the day or mornings
on the way to the next neighborhood
when we prayed for more
of ourselves to give

Labor Day Weekends at Lakeview United Methodist Campground

After pulling the hoodie over
her head, leaving it up for warmth,
she unzips the tent's flap. Morning
coolness rushes, awakening
tiny arm hairs in her sleeves.

She stuffs hands in pockets
and pads across the dirt path
to the community fire ring
at the center of the campsites.
Here parents wait for the hour
when children wake. Fathers
read newspapers. Mothers chat
with mothers. Nearly all have coffee
cups in hands, laps, or camp-
chair drink holders. The fire
from last night's roast and singing
fest is quiet now.

She drops into a chair near
her mother with a sleepy grin
of greeting. Someone asks
how she slept. With her age
and love for this weekend,
she is one of the first kids up.

A bird calls to a bird, a newspaper
folds and unfolds, wood pops
while laughing souls do not hear
the fluttering wings of forgotten
deadlines in the distance.

Gelston Hall 150

many full moons have filled the sky
since I have looked at this window

I see the ledge where my bonsai tree stood proud
in its square blue pot, pebbles encasing the trunk

I remember the futon friends would stop in
 to have a nap on while I read at my desk

with the wooden loft Dad built standing over me,
peppered by multi-color marker messages—a sort of yearbook—

and the lounging stuffed animal, King Frog, atop my tiny TV
we gathered around with pillows and popcorn on the tile flooring

and the standing closet where I hung my towel
after the morning war with community showers

and the courtyard I would gaze upon on hard days—
the spring grass, the fallen leaves, the snow-covered oak

Section III: The Everyday

Routine

I was reminded of my mother's love
as I lay in an extended wheelchair
in the kitchen, leaning
from one hip to the other
as she slid out my underwear
with its gathered plush of red
and slid a fresh set under
before the dam broke again.

After velcroing the shorts around
my pinned and pin-filled legs
and locking the seat up in place
she pulled back the curtain
separating our teamwork
from family watching
America's Funniest Videos
on the old, flower-print sofa.

6-seater Cessna

I left my corporate desk
to fly across
a corner of the country

I touch my Cessna down,
rubber fighting asphalt,
scream by the tower in this small town
to pick up a girl
young
probably pressing fingers to vending glass

she is small
        not fragile
yet broken in places

a man who knows
which hinges need screws
waits for her
in a wing with warm-painted walls
washing his hands again and again
with skin-peeling soap

Reflecting on My Place in the Cosmos

> *"In paradise, hospital beds sit under*
> *ageless mahogany and sycamore that bear*
> *every kind of fruit"*
> —Fady Joudah, Pulse 13

There are no hospitals in heaven!
    Paradise is better than any bark bed one can dream up!

        NO MORE roommates (who throw linens at nurses)
    always managing to checkout before you do,
  leaving you alone with crushed and crusted
… "food" they seem to call it
          NO MORE drip-dropping meds or pills in plastic cups
  or being handed something they believe to be toilet paper
in a "private" space that smells of bleach and sick
and they return every two hours to feel you up
    for BP and pulse checks
        and each time you think, almost aloud
  Yes, I'm still lying in this damn bed
staring across to the cream-colored wall
    at the TV with the same lame shows
          and I'm wondering if the world outside
  has CHANGED
  since I realized
    Earth is the question place,
Heaven the answer

Putty Syringed into Outer Ear Will Harden

She stares through the window,
waiting for the boop and blips
that will tell me how to adjust
her new hearing aids, what pitches
of frequency and volume will help,
not hurt, her tiny eardrums

In the sound booth, freckled by holes
like corkboard that keeps sound out,
or in, she can't hear me
until the pilot muffs are removed

I slide in the machines
with molding fit for the outer ear
made two weeks ago and teach her
how to turn them on, or up, before test
two when suddenly she is big-eyed
hearing the world

She wants to know what that sound is,
one she's never heard
in her nine years of living,
but she can't name it, can't grab it
like the paper-bag rustling it is, so close
to her—right there! that, what is that!—
sitting, twisting, stillness,
trying to hold the sound
like blue jello in her hands
when she pins it—
oh! it's my shirt
on the back of the chair!

Short Rules

short hand
short stories
short of the mark

short list
short supply
short a bit on cash

short coming
short circuit
short-distance calling

short stop
short run
short of breath

short cut
short bus
shortest path A to B

short skirt
short shorts
short-term relationship

short while
short lived
short of a miracle

The Gait Lab

for once I am a munchkin in this Kansas land gone wrong: I'm lit up, while the lights are off, with all these electrode balls stuck on my fibulas, femurs, spine, shoulders, and I'm walking the yellow brick road with this same old limp as these laser lights connect with the balls to track at what angle exactly the ankle turns out, the hip pops up, and the back strains to compensate, all so that the great Wizard can tinker with his tools behind the curtain and I'll emerge from the mansion with a better set of legs

Ty 3

Pains from my vertebrae glue
every fragment of my body
Tylenol 3—thank God for codeine—
dulls the work of the carpenters
and convinces my eyelids anchors are attached.
Ty 3, fed through one of my many plastic
octopus legs,
pumps rivers to the source
where they zipper-opened my spine
and clamped the metal poles side by side.

I want to let Mom borrow
Ty so he can shield her
from the "whore," "whore"
my father hurls at her
from across my hospital bed.

The Red Box

Sometimes during lunch or watching cartoons on the TV that hangs from the ceiling, a blood-poke lady comes to take my blood. She'll come in carrying her red box that is like a jail for all the blood she takes from kids. She'll have on one of those nurses' shirts with the happy animals all over it—hippos or cats or teddy bears in all different colors. I think it is funny she wears those shirts because she isn't as happy as the animals are.

She knows I don't like her, even though I don't mean not to like her. I make my hands into big rocks that don't open when she comes in—my fingers hiding the purple they have turned from so many pokes. Sometimes I get poked four times a day, sometimes only two times. I like those days.

I don't think the blood-poke lady likes doing the pokes. I think she has a mean boss who works in the basement of the hospital and he tells her to take the blood from kids. I am glad he doesn't do the pokes.

She comes to the side of my hospital bed. With her spidery fingers she starts to open my hands, trying to pull my fingers out. But I am strong. Mom has to help her and tells me to open my hands. She knows I don't want to.

I, Your Shield

I hugged you until you fell asleep
and they slid a tube in your throat

a nurse carried me out
through double doors

back in mom's arms
I thought of you lying there
shieldless
while they broke your body,
a sacrifice to science

mom hugged me until
we saw you again,
waking to the fight
of the long night ahead,
of tubes, beeping, blood
pokes and pressure cuffs,
of me tucked in
that space between
your hip, arm, and
a heavy cream blanket

My Halo Has Shifted

I flew over continental states
to a treatment room
hidden in a mean supply hallway
I was laid on the metal table
no medicine or pillow given me
my mom holding my hand
the nurse holding my head
Can't move, Can't cry
he said with his drill
before unscrewing the pins
and screwing them in again
earthquakes trembling
my broken body to its core
mom and my eyes latching together
to keep each other strong
as our souls made rivers on our faces
and pools on the floor

Those Little Reminders

> *"I wonder why it didn't fade, as scars are supposed to."*
> —Molly Peacock, *The Second Blush*

scars are tattoos you don't have to pay for

    except you do

and the inker doesn't ask for an idea:
just scribbles on the skin of the sleeper

I'd like to have them removed, unstitched,
these battle wounds of war

take them from my shaved legs, the hills of my hips,
the zipper up the back holding the battery pack

but then I might fall apart

    wisdom ripped like wings at the seams

Rethinking Repair

> *"Unfamiliar with the logic of the physical world, As a kid I did not understand repair."*
> —James Cihlar, Undoing

Most kids cannot
understand the logic of the world:
repairs are necessary
for the broken

I knew at eight
a body always can be dealt with,
as if a connoisseur
composed by pain

It becomes you,
a habit ingrained in inner brain,
teaching others how to think
in waves of new

You look at you,
see how the past pieces fit and click,
make a whole working puzzle
tight with glue

www.ingramcontent.com/pod-product-compliance
Lightning Source LLC
LaVergne TN
LVHW041550070426
835507LV00011B/1028